S0-EFX-200 Voice

Notes on the Art of Poetic Collaboration

by Eric Greinke

Poetry
Sand & Other Poems
Caged Angels
The Last Ballet
Iron Rose
The Broken Lock - Selected Poems 1960-1975
Selected Poems 1972-2005
Wild Strawberries
Traveling Music
For The Living Dead - New & Selected Poems

Translation
The Drunken Boat & Other Poems From The French Of
    Arthur Rimbaud

Collaborations
Great Smoky Mountains (with Ronnie Lane)
Masterpiece Theater (with Brian Adam)
Up North (with Harry Smith)
Get It (with Mark Sonnenfeld)
Catching The Light - 12 Haiku Sequences (with John Elsberg)
All This Dark - 24 Tanka Sequences (with John Elsberg)
Beyond Our Control - Two Collaborative Poems (with Hugh Fox)
Zen Duende - Collaborative Poems (with Glenna Luschei)

Essays, Interviews & Book Reviews
The Potential Of Poetry
Conversation Pieces
Poets In Review

Creative Non-fiction
The Art Of Natural Fishing

Fiction
Sea Dog - A Coast Guard Memoir

Social Commentary
Whole Self / Whole World - Quality Of Life In The 21st Century

The Third Voice
Notes on the Art of Poetic Collaboration

Eric Greinke

PRESA PRESS
Rockford, Michigan

Copyright © 2017 Eric Greinke

Acknowledgments

Some of this material first appeared in:

The Delaware Poetry Review (Lewes, DE, 2015; *Old Dogs At Play: Collaborating with John Elsberg* by Eric Greinke)

Forge - An eclectic journal of modern story, culture, and art 10.1, (New York, NY, Lincoln, NE, London, UK, 2016; *Little Novels* with Alison Stone)

Home Planet News (High Falls, NY, 2015; *Up North With Harry Smith* by Eric Greinke)

Solo Novo (Carpinteria, CA, 2015; Notes on *Beyond Our Control* by Eric Greinke)

Great Smoky Mountains (Free Press, Grand Rapids, MI, 1974; Eric Greinke & Ronnie M. Lane)

Up North (Presa Press, Rockford, MI, 2006; Eric Greinke & Harry Smith)

Catching The Light - 12 Haiku Sequences (Cervena Barva Press, West Somerville, MA, 2009; John Elsberg & Eric Greinke)

All This Dark - 24 Tanks Sequences (Cervena Barva Press, West Somerville, MA, 2012; John Elsberg & Eric Greinke)

Beyond Our Control -Two Collaborative Poems (Presa Press, Rockford, MI, 2012; Hugh Fox & Eric Greinke)

Zen Duende - Collaborative Poems (Presa Press, Rockford, MI, 2016;Eric Greinke & Glenna Luschei)

First Edition

Printed in the United States of America

ISBN: 978-0-9965026-6-5

Library of Congress Control Number: 2017941016

PRESA PRESS
PO Box 792   Rockford MI 49341
presapress@aol.com   www.presapress.com

The Third Voice
Notes on the Art of Poetic Collaboration

Contents

Chapter One - The Third Voice

When poets collaborate, the personae of their poems transmutates into a third voice, which is the combination of their individual voices. The poem they produce together is no longer the product of a single personality. It takes on a social aspect, even within the limitations of a duo.

Additionally, the process of composition is no longer driven by the repertoire of a single poet. There is interaction that constantly informs the creative process itself, transmutating it in motion.

As the creative relationship progresses between collaborators, so does the interpersonal. The poems that collaborators produce together are, in effect, a by-product of the interpersonal relationship.

It can also work in the opposite manner, with the driving energy coming from the poems to the poets. These are not mutually exclusive, so eventually the energy flow is circular, coinciding with the emergence of the third voice.

The potential for aesthetic tension is greater in a collaborative work. Poets may try to amuse, negate, confirm, surprise and tease each other while composing together. Aesthetic tension is an element that is essential to the full realization of any work of art, including poetry.

Age and gender differences may provide a widely divergent dialogue between the participants, and the divergency is passed through their poems to their readers, who experience the third voice only. A fresh new voice emerges as collaborators work toward a completed poem which is a balance of both their talents and thematic concerns.

Greater than the sum of their parts, collaborative poems represent an evolutionary leap in the art of poetry.

Universality has been the traditional goal of great literature. Collaborative poetry achieves a level of universality that is greater because it is a social rather than a personal artifact.

Bean Spasms

Ted Berrigan's collaborations with Ron Padgett, *Bean Spasms* (Kulchur Press, NY, 1967), were widely influential on my generation of poets. The poems were entertainment, pure and simple. The energy of spontaneous composition propelled them. Their use of colloquial language and topical references was quite liberating to us at that time.

Berrigan and Padgett began collaborating for their own entertainment, usually while waiting for dinner to be ready. They'd take turns adding a mixture of quotations from books, overheard conversations, phrases from the radio and other diverse material into collage-like poems. Then they'd read them aloud, for everyone's amusement. I suspect that the laughter came as much from the liberating freedom of the 'anything goes/collage' approach than from any intrinsic humor in the material itself.

They called the file-folder of their collaborations *Lyrical Bullets*, a satirical transmutation of the famous collaboration between the English Romantic poets Samuel Coleridge and William Wordsworth, *Lyrical Ballads*.

Poet friends who came by during collaborative writing sessions would add their own lines. *Bean Spasms* included short plays, a fictitious correspondence, a section of a novel, fictitious interviews, mistranslations of French poems, parodies of their own and other's poetry, and cartoons by their friend, artist Joe Brainard.

The fearless experimentation of *Bean Spasms* sent an important message to the next generation. We felt that we had been given permission to have fun with poetry. Berrigan and Padgett brought a real and much needed joie de vivre to poetry, and it was as contagious to the Boom

Generation as the earlier liberating influence of the Beat poets.

In the early seventies, poets Ben Tibbs, Ronnie Lane and I enjoyed reading aloud from *Bean Spasms*, very probably in circumstances similar to those within which the poems were composed, as either after dinner entertainment, or during our bull sessions about poetry. (We were the core of the local poetry avant-garde in Western Michigan and met frequently at each other's homes as part of an ongoing dialogue about poetry. Other poets, such as Dave Cope, Robert Swets and Barbara Robbins, also attended these sessions sporadically.)

After we got into *Bean Spasms*, we advanced to writing our own collaborations. I collaborated most often with Ronnie Lane, and soon we had a collection of pieces, which we published as *Great Smoky Mountains* (Free Books, Inc., 1974).

Great Smoky Mountains

My first collaborations with Ronnie Lane were simplified versions of what we thought Berrigan and Padgett had done in *Bean Spasms*. Their compositional methods were much more divergent than ours. We simply alternated lines. We also 'took permission' from the older poets of *Bean Spasms* to have fun by spontaneously saying anything with little or no self-censorship.

Ronnie and I were very similar in many ways: high school friends with similar social/economic backgrounds, gender, age, likes and dislikes. When the two poets in a collaboration are so similar, it creates a different tone and voice than those produced by a more heterogeneous collaborative pairing. In our case, it mainly produced fun and silliness. But it was liberating nonetheless, at that point in our development.

The other influence on our collaborations at that time was our exposure to Dadaism and Surrealism. I first got into surrealism as a mid-teen, through the paintings of

Salvador Dali. Surrealism was only a short step from my original artistic orientation of abstract expressionism. I discovered literary surrealism as I entered my twenties and was excited by its possibilities.

Like Berrigan and Padgett, we read our collaborative poems aloud to our wives and anyone else who happened to be there, to great laughter. The stranger they were, the more we liked them.

The lack of seriousness was a reflection of our preexisting relationship. Ronnie and I kept up a running comedy dialogue throughout high school and college. Humor was our third voice and mode. Thus, our work reflected our relationship.

The poems in *Great Smoky Mountains* were all fairly short. Later, Ronnie Lane and I collaborated on several longer pieces, but never published them beyond a small litmag. (*Midnight*, Memphis, TN). I lost my last copy several years ago before my archives were better organized.

Here are some typical examples of the poems in *Great Smoky Mountains*:

Bath Ornament

Lay down. Chew dead calendars.
Drink Pancreas Tea.
Eat libraries.

Dust egg yolks in transit
Under fur lined gulls.

Plant a platter of meat
On your thoughtless knees.

My pen drools incest!
My Grace dances in the soupy pie!
My teeth light up!

Afternoon

She had more teeth than some.
Such abuse

ignores   as hallways

the lunch on the patio.
Letters stare now,
to a useless ramp.
She resigned herself to chase an animal.

* * *

Music

Beards of loneliness
Cancers of delight
Drain into the afternoon
Into the open fields
Of the lost caravan.

Layered hides of plastic
Play outside my hair
While tiny silver darts
Cross the canyons of brains that dot the heart
Like an umbrella or a red violin.

* * *

Grand Haven

Fly to the red sun:
hold gravity in your bed
hold your dead in sounds
hold sound in your eye

We 'invented' a form: one-line poems with titles. These little poems were put in a sequence, *Vestibules Of Hell*, included here in its entirety.

Vestibules Of Hell

THE WINDMILL
There is a difference.

THE BIG DOG
So life went on.

BLACK SUN
The police commandeered the computer.

MAD DOG KILLS FOUR
This conviction was not of a religious nature.

STREET RUMORS
The top hat on the wall fascinated him.

GEORGE WASHINGTON
It's hard to talk about.

TOMB
My father on ice like the hats.

BEHIND A DOMINO
"The towers in this wind are laughing."

THE PAINTED CRIME
The musk-ox floated roughly toward town.

THE DEAD SURFER
The girl rose on delicate wings.

CURTAIN OF BLOOD
Busses in ballet clothes.

TAMBOURINE
The poor box was empty.

CONSTANT REMINDER
You put that back!

FRAME UP
Castles In The Sky

SCARE IN THE SUBURBS
Honk If You Know Jesus

MASTURBATION
Hollow gourds rattle.

EVERY MAN
He winks in the mirror.

PTOLEMY
Tigers were swarming over the wall.

SECRET DESIRE
I have to get a haircut.

BIG SCREAM
Black bird on a telephone wire.

LUST
Red foil.

HUNG JURY
I was fixated on her tits.

ASPECTS OF ARCHITECTURE
Her braces gleamed in the fire.

CROWN OF CREATION
The worm crept from the bag.

SCENES IN THE FOG
Doors open & close.

NIGHT CREATURES
Alcoholics, moonbeams & mathematics.

HIDDEN PLANS
The shrunken head laughs.

TEA
The secret was between us.

RUSTY LEAVES
"Leave It To Beaver"

IRONING BOARD
No one ever agreed on anything.

CHEAP PUBLICATION
They gave it away.

BOA
t hook.

ORIENTAL EXPRESS
Gently down the stream.

I learned several valuable lessons from my first collaboration with another poet. Poetry does not have to be product oriented. It can be process oriented. A certain unity is achieved simply through inclusion. The elements of a poem can be unrelated, in a linear sense, yet related through the simple act of juxtapositioning them together in a poem.

I already knew that poetic Dadaism was a "noble failure" because each individual word has meaning. The Dadaists tried to create meaningless poetry, but readers persisted in finding meaning in it anyway. Putting words together in a random manner doesn't eliminate their meaning. It may even enhance meaning to randomize words, because ambiguity and mystery challenge the gestalt function of the human mind that forms meaningful figure-ground concepts. Dadaistic poetry, often referred to as 'word-salad,' is not meaningless. It's just more complicated than poetry that is based in traditional, linear narrative and syntax.

The most important principle I learned is that one plus one equals three. When two poets collaborate, a third voice is created.

This book examines the several major factors that influence the formation of a collaborative third voice in poetry. Unlike the early beginnings described above, the collaborations that follow lasted years and were undertaken in partnerships with already accomplished older poets. Chapter Two, *Up North*, is about my collaboration with Harry Smith. It focuses on parallel dialogical collaboration, a form where poets write whole poems independently but in specific response to each other's poems.

Chapter Three, *Old Dogs At Play*, is about my evolving collaboration with poet John Elsberg, which began in parallel form, arranging each other's haiku into sequences which we published anonymously, and developed into a second project of tanka sequences where we wrote each other's titles and arranged each other's sequences. We began a third project wherein we composed poems together using a new form that we invented, a hybrid of Japanese forms, but John died before we could finish it.

Chapter Four, *In Deep,* about collaborating with Hugh Fox, describes my intensely emotional collaboration with a fellow poet with terminal cancer.

Chapters Five and Six recall my lengthy cross-gender and generational collaborations with elder poet Glenna Luschei and younger poet Alison Stone, the most widely divergent of my partnerships.

Although every combination of partners has not been tried, I have learned several principles that apply to the collaborative process which I hope will encourage other poets to collaborate. Shared creativity gets us out of our own individual egos and concerns into the larger picture.

The third voice is born through the projections of the collaborative poets. The third voice may be a freer spirit and freer verbally and mentally too, than the individual poets are alone. The potential of poetry is expanded then, for the participants and for the Art itself.

Collaborations between two poets can come in varying degrees of interaction and integration. In my collaboration with Harry Smith, we wrote poems in response to each other's poems. The poems were written individually, but they related to each other through subject, setting and what is best described as spirit.

The idea was to evoke the feeling of being 'up North' through description. Harry's 'up North' was Maine. Mine was Michigan's Upper Peninsula. Harry was in the process of moving from NYC to live full time in Maine. I had lived in the Upper Peninsula as a young Coast Guardsman, back in the sixties, and had visited there most summers since.

I had a long history with Harry. We had first been published together in 1971 in Menke Katz's *Bitterroot Quarterly Poetry Magazine*. So, I knew him first as a fellow poet. Later, I became aware of Harry's publishing activities with *The Smith* and related publications like *Pulpsmith* and *Newsletter On The State of the Culture* and others. I also knew Harry in the seventies in his capacity as President of COSMEP, the first national association of small literary publishers. My own press back then, Pilot Press Books, was an early member of COSMEP. Harry and I became closer as contributing editors for *Inside The Outside - An Anthology of Avant-Garde American Poets*. Following that big project, we worked together again as contributing editors, along with Hugh Fox, of *Presa* literary magazine.

Although I spoke to him for many hours on the phone, I never met Harry in person. When we spoke on the phone there were no silent breaks. We often interrupted each other, two dominant males who both liked to opinionate. There was plenty of interpersonal warmth between us, but there was always a dialogue. Our phone calls usually lasted over two hours. Harry was well-known for his strong opinions. He was an iconoclast and a generalist. He was a great story teller, and loved to illustrate his points with his experiences.

Our phone conversations were often about our non-literary shared interests; dogs, fishing, gardening and small boats. Harry was partial to border collies, and his dogs were rescued from shelters. He loved fishing, but didn't hunt. He loved to hoe his vegetable garden. He preferred to grow his own vegetables, or buy them from local farmers. He had a double-ended surfboat like the one I'd trained on in the Coast Guard. We both loved small boats. This kind of sharing was essential to our collaboration. I once told him that I considered him my big brother. It was a sentimental moment between us.

Our first attempt at collaboration produced a two-person broadside. My poem, *The Run*, dedicated to Harry, is a response to his poem *The Rites of Fall*.

Rites of Fall

I play each season's major symphony.
Its odors & tastes, colors, sights & sounds.
Now autumn & I meld a tapestry
Of life's slow burning, and the earth abounds
With fecund decay. I shall oxidize
Like blazing leaves. I shall be as eiswein
Sweet-tempered by the frost while the vine dies,
Or apples over-ripe: a rich design
Of rot & renewal, preparation
For the spring surge. I shall become compost.
Composition & decomposition
Are one, which is why I love the fall the most.
I fall laughing into soft sphagnum moss
Of fog forest: there is no waste, no loss.

The Run
for Harry Smith

We cannot hope
When the white flame is gone
That other fires don't burn
Under the flags of ancient ice
Beneath the tears of regret
Beyond the edge of light

Far from their overheated dens
Cold men run to the end
Down the darkened passing lanes
To strange gardens of fire
In wombs where they began
Beyond the porcelain moon

We'll feel no pain for what we've been
Even if it's never spring again

Both poems are sonnet variations, Harry's is more formal than mine. Both poems address the subject of life after death. They are apparently complimentary but there is a subtle difference in their scopes. Harry's poem addresses the processes of the earth as a microcosm, whereas mine addresses death from a macrocosmic perspective.

Our first collaboration set the format for the *Up North* series that followed. One of us sent a poem and the receiving poet wrote a poem in response, creating a conversation in poetry.

This type of collaboration could be called 'dialogical.' It differs in several significant ways from the collaborative practice of two poets working together on the same poem.

In a dialogical format, the 'parts' have greater personal integrity. The individual poems are realized poems in their own right. The writer of the first poem sets the tone and general subject. The responding poet must decide whether to compliment the other poem as a harmony or react to it as a counterpoint, two opposite but equally appropriate responses. Several variations are possible. A poem can agree in spirit but differ radically in tone and/or style. Or, it could mirror the tone or style of the first poem but differ from it in spirit or message, or there can be more subtle effects.

Harry Smith had extensive experience in the dialogical approach to collaboration. In 1981, he had published *Two Friends* with Menke Katz, which was followed up by *Two Friends II* in 1988.

Menke was the editor of *Bitterroot* and author of ten books of poetry in Yiddish and three in English. He had doctorates in both theology and modern poetry.

The *Two Friends* collections were the products of over a decade of regular collaboration between Harry and Menke. In them, they created an ongoing dialogue, with their poems responding to each other on over seventy subjects.

In free, formal and prose poetry, their subjects ranged from the nature of God and Creation to vegetarianism. (Menke was a vegetarian and Harry an avid fisherman.) Harry proposed a similar collaboration with me in 2006. The process took about six months, with each of us writing fifteen poems.

Example 1:

Axes

What is more basic than an ax?
The stone ax preceded our species.
(no stanza break)

the Neolithic hunter's fine-flaked flint,
the Olmec or Maori warrior's sharp jade,
the Sumerian's copper for war or wood,
the woodsman's iron ax from Before Christ,
the Viking raider's awesome battle ax,
the ice ax, the ship carpenter's, the cooper's,
the butcher's, the wheelwright's, the
    coachmaster's,
and all the felling & hewing axes
like Canada broad, Georgia long bit,
Michigan, Ohio. Kent, Kentucky,
New Jersey, Pennsylvania and Hudson Bay,
different bits of such varied lengths & widths.
The big old double-bit ax adorns the barn,
too tricky & dangerous for me to wield.
I use the shorter head long-blade Maine ax -
simplest. Can't say I'm good enough to prove
the saying, "A good ax is a good friend."

* * * * *

Swiss Army

My favorite tool
Is not too heavy,
Not too light.

It's served me food,
Fished out lost knots,
Revealed the intricacies

Of nature, under
Its magnifying
Glass, & more.

Sometimes,
It was my only knife.
From Cape May to

Keweenaw Bay,
I reached for it
Often,

Grateful
For all my trusty
Attachments.

Example 2:

Carpenter Ants

Why do carpenter ants decide to move,
as if on signal, out of the old walls
in many companies throughout the house?
Approached, they form motionless dense circles,
disguising themselves as knots in the pine planks.
Menaced, they disperse in all directions --
elusive, quick. Is this intelligence?
And what impels these forays from the nest
on a certain summer day? Do they march,
increase their queendom when their numbers peak?
This species domesticates the aphids,
in much the same way as we tend our cows,
to sup on their rich wholesome honeydew.
A farmer said these ants do not eat wood
but would riddle the house with their tunnels.
Injecting boric acid in the walls,
we also planted poisoned sweets outside
for workers to carry back to the queen.
We slaughtered legions in our victory,
yet I can see the future Age of Ants.

* * * * *

Black Flies

In the north woods, the black flies are as constant
& insidious as time. They circle persistently at
high speed around your head until your attention
is distracted, then they dive in for a mouthful of
your temporal flesh. Only wind & rain bring
transitory relief from their eternal onslaught.

Dialogical collaborations allow for greater
variations of style and content as a collection, but,
paradoxically, they do not encourage the poets to stretch
themselves poetically as much. They may write as they
always do, without having to adapt to another voice and
mind invading the poem. The ego-boundaries are pulled in
rather than expanded. If a third voice is achieved, it is
dialogical, which also means that there is rhetoric. The
focus is on the subject itself, which benefits from the
divergent arguments of the poems.

In the two poems in Example 1, for example,
Harry's *Axes* is an interior monologue. First, the speaker
muses on the history of axes and the different types, then
as an after note, mentions that his own ability with an axe
is questionable, and that you shouldn't use a tool that you
aren't qualified for. Harry was fascinated by antique tools
and loved to attend auctions and estate sales.

In my *Swiss Army* poem, I also praise a cutting
tool. I develop it as a symbol for being adaptable. The
poem says that 'this tool has worked for me.'

Taken together, they do share a subject which is
greater than the sum of its parts. The same thing happens
in Example 2.

Harry's *Carpenter Ants* is an ode to the
adaptability of the ants. He is mystified by how they are so

organized and also impressed by them. It's a recognition of patterns larger than man in the universe.

My poem *Black Flies* is about time, which is inevitable and unrelenting, like black flies. Taken together, the two poems are 'about' the future and the mystery of time.

Example 3:

Another example of the dialogical treatment of a subject and how it widens the understanding of it can be taken from our poems on the subject of getting lost:

Getting Lost

I've gone off course or gotten lost
not just in blanking blizzards and gray gales;
I've wandered off the well-worn ways,
even home country trails I blazed myself;
a few yards aside to left or right,
a sunless day, one might as well be far
at sea in a skiff walled by fog.
I've done that too. It's best to stop,
to wait for hint of sun, or distant sound,
a clue. Don't get yourself more lost.
You might be close to where you ought to be,
yet sailing through an inland gut,
ten yards can tear your bottom out.

To miss your turn on twisting trail can mean
ten miles of feeling like a fool,
or doom. Beware, every time Adventure
beckons you into parts unknown.

* * * * *

26

Isolated Incident

Low grey clouds
Breathed a chill warning.
The smell of ice
Was in the air.
As darkness fell
I could hear
Whispers of flakes
Falling in the dark.

Next morning,
From where I stood
On the covered porch,
A series of footprints
Led off toward
The old logging road
That climbs the hill
Behind my hidden cabin.

Someone had stopped
While I slept.
Maybe a hunter
With a head start
On daybreak,
Or did the hunted
Take a break
From the snow

Before the last cold hill?

Harry's poem tells of the ways he's gotten lost, and that it's important to stop to take your bearings when it happens. My poem speculates on the meaning of some snowy footprints, trying to bridge the gap between two isolates in an isolated winter landscape. Together, they expand the subject by coming at it from two different angles.

Harry loved F. Scott Fitzgerald's idea that a genius could hold two opposing views without cracking up.

Instead of the development of a third voice that is the combination of the individual voices of two poets, the dialogical collaboration format emphasizes the differences between them. The effect goes beyond voice to include moralistic and aesthetic differences.

The experience for the reader is more like listening to a debate than an expression of one poet, a 'third voice,' that has emerged from the voices of the collaborations.

Our poetry in *Up North* differed in several significant ways. Harry used the first person persona in 80% of his poems. I used it in 40% of mine. Harry's poems all have long, metrically formal lines. My poems have breath-based or syllabic lines of varied lengths. Harry's poems are descriptive narratives. My poems are associative and imagistic. Three of my poems are prose poems with justified margins.

The differences between the poets become the positive value of a dialogical collaboration. The subjects themselves are predominant in this type of collaboration, treated from different perspectives in either poetic harmony or counterpoint. Either way, the poets get closer, and bring the reader to a closer understanding of the subjects of the poems.

Chapter Three - Old Dogs At Play

It was in late 2006, after I'd completed a series of collaborations with The Smith (a.k.a. Harry Smith), that the idea of collaborating with John Elsberg first came to me. Harry and I had done a series of 'sympathetic poems' that reflected each other's subjects, tones and settings. We had published this set as a split chapbook. (*Up North, Presa Press, 2006*)

I had begun a correspondence with John Elsberg a few months earlier. One of my styles, which critics have frequently compared to Japanese forms, was similar to John's minimalistic, Japanese-influenced style. We shared a strong reliance on imagery. John had accepted 'a sequence' of my haiku-like poems for *Bogg*. I spoke to Harry Smith about my idea to invite John to collaborate, and he encouraged me. In May of 2007, I wrote to John, and he was enthusiastically agreeable to a collaboration and suggested we concentrate on haiku.

We had been discussing haiku values as applied to free verse in our correspondence. John suggested that we do a split chapbook project of haiku-like poems. I suggested that we put them in non-linear sequences of ten haiku to a sequence, each sequence to have a title, similar to the sequence of mine that he'd accepted for *Bogg*. We also agreed to contribute sixty haiku each to the project. Everything fell into place easily.

The final collection was comprised of twelve sequences of ten haiku each. We wanted to explore the possibilities inherent in the ancient haiku form while using contemporary language, formal innovations and cultural references. We were intrigued with the idea of placing the haiku in titled sequences, thus creating longer, non-linear, imagistic poems by combining the individual haiku. The relationship between the haiku within a sequence was associative and abstract, yet fecund with implied meaning.

John had specific ideas that he wanted to explore. Here is an excerpt from one of his early letters:

"As I sat outside tonight with the dogs thinking about the book, the rough working title that came into my head was "Pushing the Envelope." My sense is that we're collecting haiku in spirit and (modern) form, that seek the quickness/ immediacy of the haiku tradition, but that push the envelope at least a bit in terms of content, distance (abstraction), tone, development (the free association of image and statement that you mentioned, in effect pushing the traditional counterpoint) and sequencing."   (email, 5/20/07)

We began from different levels of readiness. John sent me one hundred already written haiku. I only had twenty or so to send to him. We kept all of mine and I began to write more. We cut John's group to the forty or so that were the most visually imagistic. After that, John sent me groups of new ones to select from.

John felt that I have a talent for sequencing, so I agreed to create sequences of his haiku. My selections were basically intuitive. I put haiku together that had similar images or tone, or implied a story. I also sequenced my own haiku.

We titled each other's sequences, drawn from the poems themselves, usually from the last haiku in the sequence. We also sequenced the sequences. The book begins with *Catching The Light* (haiku by John) and ends with my *Hearts Of Light*. Ironically, *Hearts Of Light* is the original sequence that John accepted for *Bogg* before we agreed to collaborate.

Because I stuck largely to the classic Japanese syllabic count while John experimented with syllabic variations, the alternating sequence arrangement had an integrative effect. Here is the title sequence of haiku by John:

Catching The Light

a starry night
suspended judgement
incubating

*

luminous bands
where hands still touch
old brass knob

*

one candle
leads to another
           this old?

*

blue grass
blue-glass vase
blue strobes on the stripper

*

she's had her chorus
now all she wants
is a perfect fugue

*

she whispers
"my pubic hair is red"
rewriting spring

*

in the future
and the past between
I loved her now

pink orchard
blue apples
brushing her hair

*

coasting to the beach
on a blue highway
buffalo farm

*

morning beach   a flash of fish   catching the light

Another innovation of the collection is our extension of the Zen value of egolessness to the format of the book. We did not identify which of us wrote which haiku, in order to put the emphasis on the work itself. This extended to the acknowledgments. We felt this enhanced the project. It's a statement: *put the poem above the poet*.

I got the idea of anonymity from the collaboration between Jim Harrison and Ted Kooser (*Braided Creek*, 2003), but our use of it was more complex than theirs. We felt that the haiku tradition itself implied a Zen neutrality. It also reflected the ease and compatibility of our writing relationship. We never rushed each other, never disagreed. *Catching The Light* took nine months to complete. Cervena Barva Press was the only publisher we sent it to. Poet-publisher Gloria Mindock accepted the manuscript right away.

The thirty-six page chapbook was published in 2009. It was reviewed by every major haiku magazine, which was gratifying. All the reviews were positive. Then, we were contacted by Ban'ya Natsuishi, the president of the World Haiku Association in Japan. Natsuishi is a major authority on haiku. He has written numerous books on the subject as well as many original haiku collections. He asked to translate some of our haiku to be featured in

Ginyu, the journal of the World Haiku Association.

We were thrilled and honored when *Ginyu* was published with twelve of our haiku translated into Japanese with the English versions alongside. (*Ginyu - International Haiku Magazine*, No. 46; World Haiku Association; Fujimi, Japan; April, 20, 2010.) We felt that making a contribution to the haiku tradition as judged by a Japanese expert was a major literary accomplishment.

We began the sequel, *All This Dark - 24 Tanka Sequences*, immediately following the completion of *Catching The Light*. It took two years. John had suggested that we also do a tanka project back when we first began our work on the haiku sequences. The idea of arranging three tanka to a sequence was mine.

As with the haiku in *Catching The Light,* we built larger poems out of smaller ones. We also tried to open the tanka form itself to new subjects and tonalities/language.

One of the interesting developments for me was our exploration of water and seaside imagery. Although we lived a thousand miles apart, we both related strongly to the big bodies of water near us (the Atlantic and Lake Michigan).

Our aesthetics were similar in many ways, and there was a subtle but distinct exchange that reverberated in each other's contributions. We were very open to each other's influence.

Unlike the previous project, we both wrote poems for the tanka project from scratch. This made the process more interactive. Once again, I did the sequencing of John's poems, and wrote the titles. John wrote about half of the titles for my sequences. The title for the tanka collection was my idea, taken from one of John's lines. My own poems were written *as* sequences. John's were written first as individual tanka, then sequenced.

As before, the process was gentle and naturally paced. Our compatibility was always a source of confidence. We felt no need to 'push the river.' The

Japanese forms encourage an essentially imagistic approach with a quietly confident tone. In our correspondence we joked about being two old poet-monks that met on a mountain path.

Early in our second collaboration, John sent me an anthology of tanka. I learned that tanka are traditionally written in three modes: lyric, narrative and imagistic. I resolved to produce three sequences of each. I found the narrative mode to be the most difficult, but was ultimately pleased with the results. John's tanka also fell into the three modes, but I don't know if it was a conscious effort on his part or just a natural one, because we never discussed this aspect. The three modes were a guideline for me, though.

Just as images of light dominate in *Catching The Light,* darkness colors *All This Dark.* Here is one of my tanka sequences that explores darkness:

The Dark Roofs

in the new darkness
the white light   of a firefly
skips   on the thick hedge
it makes us think of fairies
even though we know better

*

wet city streets   shine
under crisscrossing headlights
leftover snow   melts
into the whirlpool storm drains
we breathe the heady spring breeze

*

the low moon is huge
surrounded   by distant stars
silhouettes of trees
decorate black hills
bats whirl over   the dark roofs

Cervena Barva Press published *All This Dark - 24 Tanka Sequences,* in 2012, just months before John's tragic death. He was pleased by its publication, but unfortunately he didn't live long enough to see that the book eventually became as critically successful as *Catching The Light.*

The collaborative process evolved. When John died, we were two-thirds of the way through a third collection. We developed our own hybrid form, based on both haiku and tanka, and on the uneven metrics/syllabics of Japanese forms. These were completely interactive, with both of us contributing lines to the same poems.

In early February of 2011, I sent John a hybrid of the Japanese forms with seven lines. John responded with a seven-liner of his own. On 2/21/11, we agreed to a third project, this one to integrate our voices into the same poems. By 3/15/11, we had come up with the final form of fifteen lines divided into three stanzas of 3, 5, and 7 lines. The order of the stanzas would vary. One of us would write the seven line stanza and the other would write the three and five line stanzas. We projected the collection to eventually have thirty-six poems. We finished twenty-four of them. None of the poems have been published until now.

The records of our email correspondence, over the five-plus years that we collaborated, fill a good-sized box. In going through it, two things stand out for me. The first is that our correspondence focused a lot on metrics. Essentially, we were using Japanese syllabics, which are always uneven (3, 5, 7), to resist iambic pentameter. Our lines were also breath units. We used caesuras to break the even beats and, most importantly, to more closely replicate natural, breath-based, free associations.

The other thing I note from the correspondence is the non-poetry relationship, those personal comments about daily events like John's trips to the Eastern Shore, or my kayak trips. Building poems together led to a valued friendship despite the miles between us.

We would have done another twelve poems with the 3-5-7 arrangement. We also would have eventually given the sequences titles. Here are two of my favorites, illustrating the two stanza-orders we completed:

Sequence 8

if you say
you've seen a ghost
they'll call you
more eccentric   than you are
but what of neutrons
faster than the speed of light
white holes   matter

*

my shelf life
is longer
than my journey

*

weeds grow from cracks
in an old pier   rusted steel
upangles from white sand
two old dogs   play at waters edge
puppies at heart

Sequence 24

the sky stretches out
over clueless cities
by seas that birth   tidal waves
aimed at distant shores where
campfires blink   innocent eyes

*

a man with a metal detector
finds a penny on the beach
& does a little chicken dance

*

the sand is dimpled
in morning sun   the river
hums   without occasion
and willows drop their peals
here is no flirt   that
tide won't change
no promise   for tomorrow

In the years that I collaborated with John Elsberg, I was always secure in his warmth and patience. John had a high regard for process. I loved writing with him, because we were so compatible. Some artistic collaborations thrive on tension, but some, more sublime, thrive on compatibility. My collaborations with John were of the sublime kind.

When two poets collaborate, a third voice emerges that is greater than the sum of its parts. The new voice can lead to a state where shared symbols reveal universal truths. The effect of this on each poet's individual voice can be profound. John Elsberg's voice is a part of me now, enriching and nourishing my own. Isn't the purpose of poetry to transcend one's self?

Note on the Text

This chapter was originally written in response to a request by Amanda Newell of *The Delaware Poetry Review* for an essay about my collaborations with John Elsberg. After publication, it inspired me to write about collaborating with Harry Smith. The concept then evolved into a book project that would both memorialize and analyze my long-term collaborations.

Carnations and *Beyond Our Control* are unique poems written under unique circumstances. They were composed over the period of one year in collaboration between myself and Hugh Fox. We wrote one or two lines every day, eventually producing the 170 line *Beyond Our Control* as a blended third person voice, and the 130 line *Carnations* as a blended first person voice.

I first became aware of Hugh Fox in the early seventies, through our mutual friend Al Drake. Drake was the editor of *Happiness Holding Tank* out of East Lansing, Michigan. Fox was the editor of *Ghost Dance*, a little magazine of experimental writing. Both Al and Hugh were professors in the English Department at Michigan State University. The first time the three of us were published together was in 1972, in an anthology of Michigan writers that also included Thomas Fitzsimmons, Conrad Hilberry, Joyce Carol Oates, Ben Tibbs, James Tipton and John Woods. (*Michigan Hot Apples*, Bloomfield Hills, MI, 1972) Our mutual interest in experimental writing and in the burgeoning small press movement put us in the avant-garde contingency of the Michigan literary scene. Forty years later, Hugh, Harry Smith and I served as contributing editors to *Inside The Outside – An Anthology Of Avant-Garde American Poets* (Presa Press, 2006) and subsequently for *Presa* magazine.

The circumstance that dominated the poems was Hugh Fox's terminal cancer. He had been told that he had a year or so to live. He was having nightmares. Although he and I did not plan it, the natural subject of the poems became mortality. They are poems about death written by a dying poet and his friend. Hugh needed to work it out through poetry, and he needed help to do it. I needed to help my friend and deal with losing him.

In the end we felt that we had achieved a third voice that was greater than anything either of us had done individually. *Carnations* was first published in the *Wilderness House Literary Review* in 2010. *Beyond Our Control* was first published online in *The Pedestal Magazine* in September of 2010. Hugh Fox died on September 4, 2011. These poems were his final major works.

Hugh Fox and I wrote these two long poems over a period of one year, hardly missing a day. We wrote one line at a time, each poet writing every other line. We chose who would start each stanza intuitively and randomly. We also ended the stanzas when one of us came up with a satisfying and apt last line. So, the only 'rules' were every other line each and a first person singular blended voice for *Carnations* and a first person plural blended voice for *Beyond Our Control*. The book that resulted was *Beyond Our Control - Two Collaborative Poems* (Presa Press, 2012). An index at the back of the book identifies the first and last lines of each stanza by its writer.

The aesthetic tension in the poems comes largely from our dialogue about Hugh's impending death and how to feel about it. My effort throughout was to make it more universal and abstract, while his was to personalize it.

One reason that Hugh had difficulty staying with the third person is that his ego boundaries, which were normally much more expansive than average, began to shrink under the stress of his impending death. The reality of death as it comes closer would affect anyone's ego boundaries. I've known terminal people who became catatonic under similar conditions. It was natural enough, but not good for him.

When he slipped to first person, I'd cue him, but I didn't throw his lines away. Instead, I responded to them, in first person, then segregated them from the main poem.

These segregated lines evolved into the second poem *Carnations*.

It seems, on the surface, that there is more of Hugh in *Carnations* and more of me in *Beyond Our Control*. This is a credible view, but not a complete one. When Hugh was in the third person groove, he rocked. His third person lines are better in *Beyond Our Control*. It is true, though, that I wrote the first and last lines of *Beyond Our Control* and Hugh wrote the first and last lines of *Carnations*.

Sometimes we each wrote several lines in a given day. The communication was intense, because Hugh was a 'compulsive pen pal.' He wrote daily to several close friends, including Glenna Luschei, Richard Kostelanetz and A. D. Winans. As I noted previously, Hugh possessed an expansive ego under normal conditions. He maintained it nicely during the decade he fought cancer. It was only in the last two years that his ego boundaries began to shrink.

These two poems were Hugh's final major projects, and we were both gratified and elevated by our collaboration. Hugh had an enormous capacity for intimacy. Collaborating intensely over such a long period of time was an experience in closeness that I'll always treasure. We both felt that the final products resolved both our stylistic and moral issues in a unique way that neither of us could have done alone.

Hugh lived to see both poems published in magazines. He lived to see *Beyond Our Control* both widely circulated and nominated for a 2011 Rhysling Award. Since its original publication, the poem has been reprinted six times. The poem was nominated for a Pushcart Prize in 2015. I reprint it again here because it is the finest example of my collaborative work.

Beyond Our Control

The first thing we saw upon arrival was
the salamander legs and bat black eyes
that emanated from a face of
distant stellar cold light years
that was strangely familiar
from ancient demon-goddess dreams
where eternal fire flares from onyx eyes
and the body hills and valleys whisper
secret messages from defunct deities
that resurrect in your word/dream-made-flesh
world made fresh, reborn but left
still unreachably distanced from our hungry claw
sour dry wooden legs, our feet of hot lead
and the unspeakables that have been destroyed by
our insatiable need for
not merely flesh, but a one-way escape into the world of
cosmic words, to burn like the phoenix
firebird and fire-sun town, extended old-time years of
mysterious departures, new stars and endless music
when our neolithicism neos into a final Lascaux NOW
when our geological geos into a new Magritte THEN

The perfect spruce shaded house on the edge of
sub-rural oblivion, where the loud boys
are out in the thaw warm basketball driveways
staring at the raw girls and their confused
parents who are trying to decide if it's time to
stage an orderly retreat or verbalize a warning
as they try to megathink the relationship between
greasy abandoned keyboards and feeble mountain peaks.
Ancestral valleys, streams, lagoons, earth that says
nothing but means everything, its seas awash with
memories of ancient comers and goers:
all lost islands beneath green eternity.

New season, new eyes, new whys, months of hibernation
and right back into the tragic comedy that is
the too-soon evaporation of wives, lives, prizes into
a past not so remembered as dreamt.
Trying to fashion a new Now out of the sun-bolts
that flash into the third eye
at the center of all our evolutionary divine
primetime crimes, insatiable caverns and
the Roman-Gringo U.S. empire dissolving into
noxious toxicity, cancer on the body electric.
Trying to slide back into pre-everything but
slipping instead into black holes of memory,
Polish sausaging and potato-pancaking through
memorial masquerades that mimic lost moments,
that only return in the himalayas of night. We want
only to sleep in the arms of eternal sunshine,
until the moonless moonlight of forever
washes us in the warmth of happy infinity.

Television tarts throw tantrums for our entertainment.
How about leg-smiles and evening cloud beds instead of
blaring banalities and glaring greedheads, 24/7?
Merging into the deer and wild turkey rebirthing the world,
we forget the inane strangeness of man,
move into a gunless, bombless, swordless world with
the holy animals of love, with the haloed trees and sky.
At night we climb dream-hills to the sun plateaux,
we join the spirit that stirs the stars in their migration into
this infinity that we share, going into spaces where we find
new selves in sand and storms, swimming in the growling
     wind.
Wife night in the yawn-light approaches our beds
in the black robe of love that contains every color.
Eighty four becomes forty eight, twenty four as we rebirth
     into
our own babies, tabla rasa, new into each moment.

(no stanza break)

43

Tara-star leads us down paths of enlightenment that
work like waves turning back on themselves,
washing us clean of conceptions of
love and hate, to a perfect neutral state.

Sometimes even here we'll see a calm Buddha face
in a crowd of wound-up alarm clocks, & we have to
clear off the blackboards and windows of our spirits
and send them back to the school of rockabye baby.
"C'est temps," our ancient, ancestral voices whisper,
though they chirp like hungry baby birds.
Time to put aside potato famines and guillotines,
mass mental breakdowns and apocalyptic atomic
    submarines.
Find a forest with a clear path that leads to the hills of
heaven, if you can. Find it in mind or on land.
Let the Lords and Ladies, Kings and Queens play their
    games,
changing nothing but seeing self-portraits everywhere, they
forget the plow, the prow, the expansion into
the depth of loved eyes, the soaring heights of
history erased by today's irises, poppies, rain, hands, legs
that carry us through the insanity of human conceit
into the why-wherefore-why not heart of TO BE,
despite the dry, bare ground where no seed
falls, and if it did it would squirm a moment and then
burst into an infinite explosion of rebirth, endlessly
screaming "More, more, more!"

The music of the spheres caresses our ears,
the wind off the lake caresses our faces.
So what gives with all the caressing?
The message is clear, not bullhorn rips nor
bulldog nips, nor Bette Davis lips. But,
night sky skin that whispers
secret sacred songs into our bulls eyes.

                    (no stanza break)

44

The reincarnation of a million years of Celtic, Slavic,
    Mosaic
Beatific Platonic essences, blossoming red poppies in our
hands, waiting for the right Incarnation to hand them to.

Floating through the night, the soul returns at daybreak.
We begin the journey through guava-oatmeal, cappuchino
morning still wet with dream memories,
facing another in one of the hundreds of eat-spots
that line these nostalgic streets, these streets of
Falafal and Hot Dogs, Tacos and Bulgarian chicken wraps,
Mongolian barbecue shacks and premature heart attacks.
Loving the old, old ladies with their white hair, skinny legs
that came so far, their eyes reflecting lost desire.
At last having come to terms with Reality, opening up their
minds to realize that every minute counts, they
are incarnations of the Great Mother goddess who dwarfs
even the phallic mountains in her sphere of love.
We begin again and again our-towning it the best we can,
but the play turns to end-game, waiting for Godot,
who still doesn't come as terrace-overlooking-the-river day
old-man, but instead a cosmic femininity, a presence of
flowers and hills and forests, lakes, ponds, wide acres of
holy lifeblood water, shining out to space.
It wraps its cosmic presence
around each floating soul, newborn but old.

C'est temps for hands and eyes, tongues and bodies
    stretched
from seed to sea, currents flowing through the body
    electric,
the mind expanding out of cybernetic screens into the
    warbling,
warping net of omnipotent time, and farewell to
rhino-crocodile fanged-clawed murdering man-woman,
and good-bye to schizophrenic train wrecks and

(no stanza break)

45

unsympathetic tsunami,
unbreathable downtowns and the Thornton Wilderless
    evening news.
Gone the pale pastel rooms festooned with fading family
    portraits,
antique grandmas papriking red-onioned beef into taste-
    bud ecstasy,
newborn babies bawling their protests against the
    sudden light.
School, graduation and the next generations come,
and then they're gone, sand scattered on the big beach.

We have been carried along by a flood of songs,
mostly in languages we didn't understand as the audio-
    visual world
wasn't our reality, but the melodies played around us as
wind-tree bird-song thunders that brought us back to
    our real selves,
yet forward and away from our selves too, into a long
immersion in the sensual celebrations of
sub-atomic love down ancient genetic pathways.
We move into nightly realland-dreamland and march
    along
the long black highway of history, our voices histrionic
    and
filled with Finnegan brogues and shmoozing with
Quixotes that joust with the vibrant windmills of
    memory.

The spirits of our ancestors waft around us,
haunt our whys and why-nots, wherefores and where-
    nexts,
remind us that soul music is in us all,
and the evening disaster-news has nothing to do with
the neutral universe that neither loves nor hates us.
Simply BEING here on the Galileoan earth as it

(no stanza break)

is enough, even though the celestial warbling stops
  before
the great silence at the center, where nothing
but memories take off for their v-shaped migrations into
a south beyond the frozen pole of this poor planet.
Never thinking about asteroids, decreasing planet-
  weight,
nor black holes that suck up whole living galaxies,
we somehow believe that our cattails and ancient ruins
  are not
illusions, due to circus stanzas beyond our control.

     Obviously, the circumstances under which *Beyond Our Control* was written were both extreme and unique. A 'perfect storm' of many factors led to its birth. I think that the major factor in play was our compatibility. We were both very intuitive, and always had very open communication. We could criticize each other without either of us becoming defensive. We genuinely admired each other's work. Above all, we both knew that the best thing we could do in the face of Hugh's impending death was to write a poem about it. But 'about it' doesn't quite get it. We were in it.

     I think about death every morning when I wake up, and when I go to sleep at night too. I think it's healthy for several reasons, but primarily because it puts a more realistic perspective on life. Each day could be my last, and yours too.

     Working with Hugh brought a new element of catharsis into the collaborative process for me. Hugh was in real anguish. He loved life, and he put it all into our poems. Though the poems have integrated voices, they are also dialogues between us.

     As an ex-psychotherapist, I recognized that our collaboration had many of the features of psychotherapy sessions, such as transference and counter-transference, where the participants essentially over-identify with each other. Rather than interfering with the poetry, this actually enhanced it. (In psychotherapy it doesn't work that way.) The third voice that emerged was highly integrated. My experience suggests that greater intimacy of personality and situations can produce a strong third voice, and in turn, perhaps a work of lasting value.

Chapter Five– Zen Duende

Following my collaborations with Harry, John and Hugh, I formed a hypothesis about poetic collaboration that mirrored a principle of great value in the practice of group therapy. As a practicing group therapist for many years, I was sensitive to interpersonal dynamics. The principle at hand is that there are two types of group compositions, heterogeneous and homogeneous. In a heterogeneous group, the members are dissimilar in gender, age, race, cultural orientation or anything else that brings a fresh perspective into the group's dynamics. The benefits of such diversity are that more divergent and creative solutions and perspectives are generated.

Homogeneous groups are composed of members who have a lot in common. They are often best when trust or manipulation are issues in the group.

I began to think that artistic collaboration functions in much the same way as group therapy, but on a microcosmic level. Interpersonal dynamics can also be understood in much the same way. Opposite personalities blend more dynamically than similar ones. (I had a musical collaboration years ago with a person of similar personality and after a while we "got on each other's nerves.")

Thus far, I had collaborated exclusively with other males of my own generation. I was ready for a different experience when Glenna Luschei invited me to collaborate in late 2012.

I began collaborating with Glenna on January 9, 2013 and completed it on September, 2015. She was aware of my history of collaboration with other poets, especially my projects with our late mutual friends Harry Smith (*Up North*, 2006) and Hugh Fox (*Beyond Our Control*, 2012).

49

Because we had both been close to Harry and Hugh, and also because of our long editorial relationship, we already shared an emotional and literary connection.

Glenna is a unique poet, in her eighties, whose poetry is recognizable for its transcendental and universal qualities, rendered in plain American speech. In a sense, Glenna's work is philosophical, as long as that term is widely defined as imagistic rather than didactic.

Her persona embodies a spiritual neutrality similar to that of Zen Buddhism. Age and wisdom have brought her to a nearly egoless state of mind. Glenna has an inner core of joy that makes her resilient in her life and her poetry.

As a younger woman, Glenna was an important leader of the small press movement. She was the first woman President of COSMEP, (Committee of Small Magazine Editors and Publishers) the primary precursor to AWP (Association of Writing Programs) of today. She is a 'crossover academic,' like Hugh Fox, Duane Locke and Gerald Locklin. These poets were renegade professors who related more to the new poetics of the avant-garde and the small independent literary presses than to academic tradition. Glenna is the publisher of Solo Press and its magazine series *Café Solo, Solo Café*, and *Solo Novo*. She is the former Poet Laureate of San Obispo, California.

In a sense, Glenna and I already had a collaborative relationship that went back a decade. I had been a very active editor of her books. Glenna is a poet who benefits from a strong editor who can draw out the themes of her work and present them in a pleasing and persuasive order.

I began working with Glenna as her editor in 2006. The result was her chapbook *Seedpods*. Subsequently, I have been the editor for three of her full length books (*Total Immersion*, 2008; *Witch Dance- Selected Poems*, 2010; and *Leaving It All Behind*, 2011) and an additional chapbook (*Sprouts*, 2011). During the past decade, I have become quite familiar with her poetry.

The degree of familiarity with each other's work is a major factor in collaboration. But, expectations may block the creative flow when collaborators know each other too well. I think it's best if the poets discover themselves and each other during the process of collaboration.

Glenna has a deep background in South American poetry. When she was young, she studied with Octavio Paz, the Nobel Laureate from Mexico whose work reflects both a transcendental universality and the influence of Nobel Laureate Federico Garcia Lorca.

Our collaborations quickly developed a range of forms and a spontaneity unlike any of my previous ones. I think this freedom of expression was due to our mutual tendency toward divergent thinking. Glenna is resilient. She's weathered life's storms and sees the big picture. Her view of life is both expansive and detailed. She's very observant of details.

Our collection *Zen Duende – Collaborative Poems* (2016) is arranged in five numbered sections. Section 1 is the long poem *Life Is*. This poem took the longest time to compose, a little over a year. Despite its placement as Section 1 of the book, it was the last poem written. The original draft was twice as long as the final version. Each of the lines is a simple metaphorical statement of what "life is." We edited the final draft by first removing non-imagistic or non-universal lines, then re-arranging the final lines to give the poem symmetry and thematic development.

We were pleased with *Life Is* as the product of our final year. For me, the poem compliments my collaborative poem with Hugh Fox, *Beyond Our Control*, which is 'about' mortality.

Life Is

spirit finding its way home

a fire in the hole

                        spinning out of control

the spatter of rain

                         orange clouds in the evening

a tree of microbes

                        hiding in plain sight

an angel dancing on the head of a pin

pewter in the tavern

a merganser consuming fish

waking to another day

                    music of the wind

a slow turtle crossing a busy highway

dirt on the mat

                    blue sky in winter

billions of planets in love

a lake filling up after drought

here & not here

                    a whirlpool of swirling souls

a sparrow huddling in a snowy hedge

a bird of prey zooming in on the sparrow

a storm heading toward shore

an algae-covered pond

young men killed in battle

a fresh egg

                    a vulture eating roadkill

a condemned man eating his last meal

rushing to meet the deadline

the uncarved block

                          a snowflake

red sky in the morning

waiting, waiting

a promiscuous tornado

a Spring breeze

                    pollen in the wind

a seagull floating miles from shore

a set of footprints outside the window

menace lurking under the bliss

dancing the Hokie pokie

a vapor trail on a blue sky

an eagle flying over open water

a slow thaw

                    polar bears running out of ice

wind over a graveyard

                              forever arriving

an orphan scrounging for food

a ewe waiting for shearing

a battle about to begin

coming out of the closet

the tea ceremony

                    a runaway train

a ship on the bottom of the ocean floor

old women who go on alone

a hummingbird crossing the Gulf of Mexico

a plume of smoke

                    a cold wind in March

going nowhere

                    carnivorous

an interconnected waterway

a surprise snow late in the season

the ones who went before

a hot breakfast on a cold morning

glass of wine at day's end

forgetting what time it is

a fight coming out of nowhere

a late snow on spring crocuses

germinating rain

                        a sparkle in a dog's eye

a song you can't get out of your head

hair salty from the ocean

the crackling of a campfire

a teenage car crash going to the prom

parents who can't afford to feed their children

a question that is never answered

a good sleep after a long walk

                                 an avalanche

dancing on the edge of a chasm

a lock with no key

        an endless feast

a beam of sunlight through dark clouds

an early crocus breaking through the snow

a murder of crows

betrayal from where you least expect it

the fiery heart of the planet

        a hard road to travel

glow of silver in the dark

ticket on the way to a funeral

dark dance of the scorpion

a hole in the fire

        flying at the speed of light

Section 2 of the book is comprised of eleven short poems, our initial efforts from early 2013. The short poem was the first format we tried. One of these (*Trout*) was printed as a letterpress broadside, hand-set by Gary Metras for Adastra Press. *Trout* is Glenna's favorite of our short poems. She used to fish for steelhead annually with her late husband Bill, who is represented as the trout in the poem, luring her to "doom."

My own favorite of the short poems in Section 2 is *Time and the Dream*:

Time and the Dream

We are at one with the other stars
Especially the ones about to explode.
I am not ready to say goodbye to this glittering
    life.
I am burning hotter than ever,
a lotus arising from filthy waters
opening my petals to the sun.
Let all the bees come here for nectar.
Let all the locks open to my keys.
It is time at last for us to enter the forbidden
    room
where the eternal amaranth still blooms.
It is time for us to hold hands, imbibe the drug.
It is time for warm blood to flow between us.
When we awake it will be on another planet.
There we'll breathe the air of dreams.

I think this poem uses imagery to imply philosophical truths without being didactic, relying on symbolism and duende. The elevated tone evokes a sense of mystical enlightenment. As the first of the short poems in Section 2, it also sets the serious baseline against which humorous and enigmatic poems such as *Cartoon* and *Ghost* could contrast.

The short poems were written without plan or stated theme. We just let them happen, each of us adding one line a day. As a result of our open compositional method, the poems grew organically and the blended voice sounds quite different from our individual styles. In such a situation, the poets are truly writing in a third voice.

Section 3 of the collection is one hundred one-line poems with titles, a resurrection of the form invented in my early collaborations with Ronnie Lane. Experience from one collaboration can resurface in another. The series is titled *Lone Bones*. We alternated every other poem, with one of us writing the line and the other the title. These were originally published in *Forge - An Eclectic Journal of Modern Story, Culture, and Art*. These little poems have a level of ironic humor. Many are enigmatic. They stand in stark contrast to the three long poems in the book. I like them because they illustrate how the juxtapositioning of a single line with a title can create an unusual but satisfying metaphor. We completed this series after the short poems, toward the end of the first year.

Here are a few examples from *Lone Bones*, some of my personal favorites:

115. VIVE LA FRANCE
Swords were integral to the decor.

126. THE ROCKIES
We knew them at their peak.

139. BIG FUN
All day I've been watching the coneflowers.

147. NOSTALGIA FOR THE INFINITE
Where blue songs warm the shallows.

151. LOOKING GOOD
Laughter bubbled over the rapids.

155. CULTURAL TREASURE
Her rose tattoo said it all.

170. PLENTY OF MEAT
It was the birth of a movement.

174. CARGO
Inside the egg was a tiny suitcase.

83. LOVE MONKEYS
But we needed the eggs

190. THE IMPOSSIBLE RHYME
He saw time wind into a bind.

194. ATTENTION TO DETAIL
Carbohydrates defeated Napoleon.

199. THE WINNER
A tiny sparrow brought the news.

Section 4 contains two long poems, *Hugh* and *Harry*. In them, we worked out our memories and feelings about our two mutual friends, who were both recently deceased. As with *Life Is*, the original drafts were approximately twice as long as the finals. The revision process for all three long poems was the same.

The editing phase was important because it brought out the themes that emerged slowly over the time the poem was composed. Editing also brought greater coherence to the poems. When editing is used as a second phase, it allows the first phase to be divergent and creative, "pulling out all the stops." It's important for the poets to take chances in a collaborative poem, to break out of the box into unknown territory as all serious art attempts to do.

The fifth section contains the dialogue *Zen Duende*. We included this non-poetry section to shed some light on the nature of the third voice that we achieved through our collaboration. Zen Duende was the term we invented for the philosophy of our third voice. It was a combination of both of our spiritual/philosophical orientations.

When collaborators come from radically different backgrounds, eras, and genders, the potential for a mind-expanding collaborative experience is heightened. Glenna was my first female collaborator, and I feel that the gender and generational differences enhanced our work.

My own mother was a poet, but she didn't have Glenna's gifts or width of vision. But, in a way, writing with Glenna was like writing with an idealized maternal figure. Our gender dissimilarity was even greater than our age difference. The voice we produced together has a unisexual tone, unlike either the feminine or masculine language we'd normally expect.

When I began the collaboration with Glenna, I was hoping to break away from homogeneous sameness. Nearly three years later, this desire had been more than realized, and by then I was already a year into my second cross-gender collaboration with Alison Stone. During the crossover year during which I collaborated with both Glenna and Alison, the practice of working on two collaborative poems at any given time was mentally stimulating. I'd recommend the experience to any poet who feels blocked.

Chapter Six – Rock & Roll

In February of 2014, I was invited to collaborate by Alison Stone, a younger New York poet whose poems have been published by the *Paris Review* and *Poetry*. She is also a talented oil painter. Alison's poetry is edgy, stark and direct. Her aesthetic reflects her early years on the Punk Rock scenes of New York and London. She has an M.F.A., but publishes eclectically in both university and independent magazines. I was familiar with her work as the editor/publisher of her collection *Dangerous Enough* (Presa Press, 2014). I like people who blur the usual lines, so I said "Yes."

When Alison invited me to collaborate, I was a year and a half into my work with Glenna Luschei, sixteen years my senior. I am likewise sixteen years older than Alison. The symmetry of working across gender lines that also featured a wide spread of generational divergence appealed to me because I surmised that something new about collaboration would be learned. From an interactional standpoint, my personal relationship with Alison grew proportionate to our body of work. We found our mutual voice in irony and humor, and also in a certain rock-influenced sound.

Early in our work together, we discovered a mutual love for the seminal punk-metal band the Plasmatics. I had mentioned that I often play marathons of my favorite bands, referring in passing to the Plasmatics as the band de jour. Coincidentally Alison had attended many of the band's concerts and even had parts of televisions and cars blown-up on stage by the band's charismatic vocalist Wendy O. Williams.

The punk-rock aesthetic is alive and kicking in Alison, and it informed our work with its values of spontaneity, honesty and directness. (Values which the punk-rockers inherited directly from the Beat literary movement.) We held these artistic values in common. Although I started as a musician in the sixties, my experience had been of the "Garage Band" type. The sixties and seventies garage bands were the precursors of the eighties punk bands.

During the first year of my three-year collaboration with Alison, I was also contributing daily to *Life Is*, the final long poem of my three-year collaboration with Glenna Luschei. It was interesting and informative for me to collaborate simultaneously with one woman who was just old enough to be my mother and another just young enough to be my daughter. One poet lived on the West Coast, and the other on the East Coast. Their styles were radically different. It was good poetic exercise to write a line for each of them every day. I recommend it to any poet who feels that his work has become predictable self-parody.

Alison and I wrote twenty-eight poems during our first year of collaboration, ranging from ten to sixty lines. Half of the poems (fourteen) contained a narrative. Two were prose poems. The most fully realized and successful poems had a level of ironic humor.

One of my favorites in the non-narrative mode is *Temptation*:

Temptation

If only it wasn't so dark there,
& it didn't rain there every day,
& if there were no mud slides there,
& if the animals stayed in the forest,
the people might be friendlier.
Instead, everyone was edgy, waiting
for a bus, a train, a messiah,

(no stanza break)

62

anything to whisk them away
from a place with no air, no particular
culture, the only fashion
rubber boots & sour
looks. The only industry
was a fashionable umbrella factory.
People there bought copious cosmetics
& many personal electronic devices.
Searching for pictures of far-away,
exotic places or foamy oceans
made their fantasies of escape
their only solace in light of the
storm clouds of defeat & fear
that navigated the scary sky.
Video games with danger
& explosions calmed them
for the moment, but everything
they knew was artificial.
Time for them was numerical.
No one felt particularly special.
Even love words between
couples were delivered in
a drone
only their dogs could hear.
So that's why I declined
to purchase more property there.

In working on a narrative poem with a
collaborator, surprise emerges as a primary value. If a
narrative "writes itself," it's likely to be predictable. The
narrative form is limited, because it lacks the mysterious
potential of the more ambiguous and non-linear forms
(such as the impressionistic, expressionistic, surrealistic or
image-based international forms like haiku, tanka and
ghazals).

In a collaborative narrative, the aesthetic tension

which is crucial to a poem comes from unexpected and creative plotting. In this mode, the poets frustrate and interrupt their collaborator's plot directions, in order to keep the poem fresh and to open up new possibilities.

Some of the poems evolved into serious lyrical statements. We never planned what direction the poems would go. Instead, we relied on intuitive associative leaps. One of my favorite poems in the lyric mode is *Final Heat*:

Final Heat

Summer's last stand -- the air
thickens. Children laugh and whine
in wading pools, dogs seek
friendly faces, their sweet
eyes shining with higher love.
Vegetable stands line the highways,
hand-lettered signs
promising freshness, hoping
to lure drivers on their way
to or from Home Sweet Home.
Thoughts of new school clothes
infect the suburban zeitgeist, while
parents cross rulers and crayons
off lists, shave pencils sharp
as the mean girls' smiles.
As the first accomplished maple leaves
enter their red retirement, burning
brilliantly right before extinction,
the other trees ready themselves,
the animals' fur thickens
imperceptibly. There's still time
for a few leaps into a lake,
or one last trip to a dusty
amusement park before the

(no stanza break)

64

water's chill evicts us
and the wooden
horses clip-clop away.
Long gone stars glow here
and now, light years away
from an unknown tomorrow.

Our method in our first twenty-eight poems was
simple alternation of lines. We also took turns writing the
all-important first and last lines of the poems. All of them
feature a first line by one poet coupled with a last line by
the other. Alison and I were able to achieve an integrated
voice very easily. When two poets find their third voice
quickly, it is because they are highly compatible and
complimentary in their predominant poetic values.

As in my work with Glenna, I found that sharing
personal information was a prominent feature of
collaborating with Alison. Our lines were always
accompanied by daily letters about our families and other
artistic activities. We wrote about our friends, our family
relationships, our problems and our daily lives. Our
closeness *may* have been based more on the fact that we
were both psychotherapists than on any presumptive
gender characteristic. Such limited experience can only
yield a hypothesis to be verified or refuted by other male-
female collaborators.

Another possible explanation for my own willingness
to share more personal details is that I have always found
it easier to talk in a personal way to women than men, who
tend to be less interested in personal talk. I grew up in a
house full of women. Maybe it's as simple as that. At any
rate, I found Alison easy to relate and talk to and I hope she
feels the same about me.

One obvious effect of collaboration is a process of
personal bonding that runs concurrently with the creative

process. The poems written together ultimately become symbols of the relationship. In this case, the relationship began as literary and evolved into a significantly more personal one.

After our first year and a half, Alison suggested that we try some formats with rules, to break out of the freestyle mode. We tried something completely different next, a series of titled five-line poems. The first person would write the first and last lines and the title, and the second would write the middle three lines. In the next several months we wrote thirty-one of them. The entire series was published in *Forge* (2016) under the title *Little Novels*. We both felt that it was our best work to date. It may be that the development of new forms represents a higher level of mutuality, like the private languages often invented by identical twins or social isolates. Here are some of my favorites:

Blown

After you let the dog out
he whimpered at the base of the
lightning-scorched pine.
A lone crow, it's caw the sound
of a loud drone, fluttered down.

* * * * * * *

Doppelganger

The day the mirror fought back was weird.
The kettle whistled battle hymns
and the Pekingese wolf-howled.
Oddest of all was the framed glass,
bulging with the reflection of my enemy.

* * * * * * *

* * * * * * *

Heavenly

After the giddy astronomers
celebrated their discovery of
water crystals on one of Saturn's moons,
the fundamentalists recoiled in horror.
Luckily, another shooting wiped this off the news.

* * * * * * *

Spin Doctor

Her many plates spun on wands of
fantasy, such fervent wishing almost
a religion, her costume jewelry twinkling
in desire's spotlight. The audience gasped
as she confidently removed the wands.

* * * * * * *

Divine Intervention

After the dog ate the only copy of my thesis,
I considered trading him at the shelter
for a gecko, then wrote a better paper
on how truth hides behind cliche. The dog
accepted my apology, as Co-Author.

* * * * * * *

Unscripted

The scent of strawberries reminded him
of his first love, and the time he took her
to see Ingmar Bergman's *Wild Strawberries*,
shown in the campus theater. They were
incompatible, he realized, when she dozed.

* * * * * * *

Sucker Punch

We should have let it go, but instead
we dressed it up in taffeta and spangled tights,
paraded it in front of friends who soon
wished to be elsewhere. We never
even saw us coming.

* * * * * * *

The Beaten

The sad marching band ran from the field, their
plumed hats drooping, out-of -tune instruments
held to their chests. They'd practiced for weeks
but their routine had been derailed by
serial love affairs in the rhythm section.

These little poems provide instant gratification for
their writers, complete in one turn each. Next, we decided
to expand the concept to twelve lines, with the first poet
writing three lines initially, the second poet six lines, and
the first supplying the last three lines and the title.

Here's an example of our twelve-line form that
illustrates its use for a narrative:

Bad Actor

The gunman surprised us
when he leapt out on stage.
His eyes were cold as he took aim
at the man in the front
row loudly unwrapping
caramels, instead of at the actor
pretending to menace
the tied-up mayor and his wife.
The other actors froze
and the audience thought it
part of the show, even after
the real blood began to flow.

This versatile little form can also be used for a short lyric statement:

Substitution

The musical milk is flowing
down into our mouths. Why pay
when you can get it free? Why
shell out a hundred bucks
for some fame-bloated rocker
when every park has
a bandstand, and there are
herds of wannabes happy
to give it away? We drink
weak skim milk
and call it cream,
watch reruns when we dream.

My final project with Alison was based in her suggestion that we do something both structured and open-ended. I suggested a question and answer format.

Our working title for the first draft was *Q & A*.

We began the project on September 20, 2016 and ended it on February 27, 2017. The original draft contained 358 lines. The contents deviated wildly from philosophical or metaphysical to music and nature. I wrote the first line. After that, we would answer the question, then ask one to start the new couplet. The third voice that emerged had the effect of deconstructing itself, since the structure encouraged the constant introduction of creative new questions. Alison and I had found that aesthetic tension is increased through diversity, irony and humor.

When we edited the first draft of *Q & A*, we took all the couplets out of context and put them in thematic categories, completely deconstructing the original. In the third draft, we reordered the thematically compatible couplets into eight shorter poems. Here is the lead off poem in the series:

1. Noise

What kind of fool am I?
The kind with stars for buttons, seas behind your
    eyes.

Are the oceans tired?
No, they're just distracted.

What is your real name?
I've looked, but I can't find it.

Where can I find love?
In dreams.

What have you lost?
Nothing.

What hides in your heart?
Ghosts.

What does your silence hide?
The noise of the universe

Where are you going?
I'm going to sleep.

I think *Noise* is a good example of how we each tried to challenge the other in both questions and answers. The natural tension in a collaboration between two (or more) distinct and creative artists may and should be transformed into the aesthetic tension necessary for a realized poem.

When we had written more than enough poems for a book collection over three plus years, we decided to end our collaboration. I edited the book manuscript at Alison's request and she came up with the title at mine, which she also agreed to illustrate for the eventual book cover. I was very pleased that she consented to do the cover art because I loved her vivid oil paintings.

The title we agreed to was based in our mutual love of raw rock music and Wendy O. Williams, the late lead singer of the seminal punk-metal band The Plasmatics. The title reflects our "anything goes" style and spirit, ironic, rebellious and provocative. We called our collection *Masterplan*, after an early Plasmatics' song.

Alison thinks that many poets secretly want to be rock stars. I think the rock and roll metaphor works for our poems because they share more aesthetic values with that music than they do with the dominant styles of contemporary poetry. The Plasmatics were famous for their radical stage act, which included sawing television sets in half and blowing up Cadillacs. The content of their songs was anti-materialistic and anti-establishment.

As I write this, Alison is planning her cover painting, which will feature members of the Plasmatics sledge-hammering a television set, an image that embodies our collaborative aesthetic.

As with John Elsberg, compatibility emerged as the greatest factor in my collaboration with Alison Stone. Because our third voice seems to have a life of its own, it may refuse to be quiet. We will have to wait and see, because above all, collaborating is *process*.

It's been nearly twelve years since the collaboration with Harry Smith that begins this book, a long period of shared creativity that nourished my appreciation of poetic diversity and expanded my individual work. Beyond that, each of my collaborators has become a part of my poetic consciousness, a great gift that keeps on giving.

1. Tense & Persona

If the use of the first person by two poets creates a third voice that is the combination of them, greater than the sum of its parts, what happens when this third voice speaks in the third person? The differences are significant, and must be viewed from both the reader's and the writer's perspectives to fully understand them.

A reader reading a first person voice that was created by two poets perceives the voice as that of a single poet who is speaking for himself or herself. But this is not real. The words in a collaborative poem represent *themselves* rather than they do the individual poets, because they are the result of a social act and also a trick. They are pretending to represent one poet, but they do not in actuality do so. The collaborative poem is, above all else, a *compromise*. It is artifice. The reader may well prefer this compromise to the purer, rawer, more direct poetry of a single individual, depending on how individualistic that poet is, of course.

When generic poets whose poems can't be identified by a unique style collaborate, the third voice effect is less of a compromise. This is not necessarily good.

From the reader's perspective, reading a poem in the third person persona written by a single poet, requires a greater metaphorical stretch. One person *can* speak for us all, but it requires a rare personal clarity to be the wise sage who does so with credibility. Great poets extend the personal and subjective to the universal, *more objective* level of meaning. Perhaps 'less subjective' would be a better term. Statements made in the third person must ring true to the general human experience, transcending gender, racial, social and cultural differences. However, when these poetic statements do not ring true, they are like loud farts at a funeral.

From the poet's perspective, writing in the first person is the easiest, most natural mode, yet the most difficult in a collaboration. Turning an 'us' into a 'me' is like alchemy; a great idea that never quite worked out. But, poetry is a form of magic, and a third voice can emerge from two individual voices. The poets must compromise well together. It is their very differences which create the energy that evolves then emerges as the third voice, credible as a 'artificial' first person. The poets' differences become reconciled in the poems they write together, and even more so in the response of the 'fooled' reader. When two poets write in the third person voice, it is less of a stretch, is more natural, and is not as artificial as two poets writing in the first person.

A plural voice is achieved through more than the use of the third person voice. It is in the values represented, in the content. The poet's attention shifts from the task of pretending that two poets are really one, to a focus on the veracity of the content. The question becomes 'Are the statements in the poem philosophically true for each of the poets?' Beyond that, will the content of the poem resonate truthfully and believably in the reader?

2. Interpersonal Factors

The depth and degree of interpersonal connection in a poetic collaboration is also largely dependent on the format of the collaboration.

In a dialogical collaboration such as my collaboration with Harry Smith, there is no development/emergence of a "third voice." My connection with Harry as a collaborator was more intellectual than emotional, with each of us giving an individual response to the objects we wrote about (cutting tools, insects,

74

landscapes, etc.)

On the other hand, my collaboration with Hugh Fox was deeply personal for a number of reasons that include not only a mixed voice but also a subject (death) that is uniquely universal as well as personal.

My work with John Elsberg evolved from parallel play to a mixed persona. *In Catching the Light*, the collaboration was more in the editing of haiku written individually than in the composition of the haiku. We did help each other with the titles of edited sequences, which each contained ten haiku. In our second collaborative project, *All This Dark*, we integrated our contributions to each other's tanka more than we did in *Catching The Light*. In the final project, which we were working on when John died, we invented our own form with aspects of both haiku and tanka and a complex revolving syllabic structure wherein each poem contained both our personae. It will be no surprise to the reader that John and I became progressively closer as our poetic voices became more integrated.

My subsequent collaboration with Glenna Luschei was initiated by Glenna because I had collaborated with our two mutual friends Harry Smith and Hugh Fox. She wanted to connect with the process that I had gone through with Harry and Hugh, and also to work through their loss. The results were our poems *Harry* and *Hugh*.

I felt closer to Alison Stone as our work proceeded and we shared personal information almost daily. I think our understanding of each other's lives contributed to the evolution of our mutual persona and the ease with which we developed our third voice.

Once again, the relationship between form and function is apparent. To use an automotive metaphor, some collaborations bang along on three cylinders while others purr on all eight. The differences depend on the match between format and content, and interpersonal compatibility combined with diversity of style.

3. Regional Differences

Regional dialects are incorporated into the sound and feel of a poem. In collaborating with poets from both coasts, my upper-Midwest dialect contrasted with theirs. If the dialectal differences are too great, it can result in a choppy, somehow foreign-sounding third voice. This can be both good and bad.

Novelty and diversity are both positive values in poetry. In this sense, dialectic differences can be creative and interesting. It seems to be a matter of degree. Too much disparity could make the third voice schizoid or off-putting. The blend is probably as important to the overall flow of a poem as is the fresh use of language.

4. Gender Differences

In my five year "experiment" collaborating with two women, I discovered the obvious. Women have greater personal comfort with sharing personal details than men do, and male poets are not the exception to gender stereotype that they often believe themselves to be. It has often been said that opposites attract. My past experience as a marriage counselor confirms this folk wisdom, with one caveat: to be compatible, couples must indeed have opposite personalities, but more importantly, they must share similar values. The type of activity doesn't matter so much as the shared values, be it poetry, marriage or social work.

In my twenty-five years as a social worker, I worked primarily with female social workers because I specialized in therapy with children. My female colleagues were extremely open about their personal lives and sociable well beyond what I experienced in the U.S. Coast Guard, which was nearly all male in the mid-sixties when I served. This is, of course, completely anecdotal evidence and should be considered merely a strong hypothesis until more male-female (and other cross-gender) collaborations can be examined and analyzed.

I will admit that the age factor also played into my relationships with both Glenna and Alison. I had fleeting feelings of working with my mother with Glenna and my daughter with Alison, but they never predominated.

5. Generational Differences

Each generation has its unique experiences, customs and shared values. These have an impact on a collaboration between two poets who are separated by a generation. Specific examples of the age-gap factor are difficult for me to recall at this point, but there was occasionally a recognition of it, primarily in the ability to make associative "leaps." Although Glenna had practiced a style of poetry that features associative leaping, age made her more concrete than Alison, who may well have felt the same effect from me. We become less abstract as we age.

Youthful energy is also a factor. Alison generally returned her lines faster than I did. However, as with gender differences, individual traits and aptitudes probably contribute more as a factor than either gender or generational differences. Further observation is needed in both areas.

6. The Play Factor

To a poet, a collaboration often has a greater entertainment value than an individual poem, because the participation of two poets makes it more dynamic. Participants are more likely to think "outside the box" and try things that they would hesitate to use in their individual work. The poets challenge each other, often in witty ways. Unexpected narrative turns and imagery exercise the imagination, which can atrophy in a closed system defined entirely by individual taste, themes and style. It is liberating to get outside one's own ego.

The first collaborations I did, with Ronnie Lane, were purely based in entertainment. Together, we experienced the joy and fun of playing with words. If a poet has lost the joy of wordplay, I suggest that a lively collaboration may be the antidote. Even if "great" poetry is not created, collaboration has wonderful value as rejuvenation and entertainment.

7. Aftereffects

Each time a poet collaborates with another poet, individual poetic growth occurs. The experience of the collaboration becomes integrated into each of the participant's work. Potential has been liberated beyond individual experience.

Following my collaboration with Hugh Fox, I wrote a poem that was clearly influenced by Hugh's style. A regular correspondent commented that it didn't sound like my other work. I considered that a victory, and replied that "It does now."

Each of my collaborations had an effect on my own poetry. I hear echoes of them in my new poems, but the echoes still feel authentically personal because they have been integrated through the collaborative experience.

8. Situational Engagement

In collaborations such as *Beyond Our Control* (with Hugh Fox) and *Harry* and *Hugh* (with Glenna Luschei), the poets engage with active life situations. Because Hugh was dying, we engaged over the subject of mortality. Because Hugh Fox and Harry Smith died, Glenna and I engaged over their loss in a way we felt brought us a kind of "poetic justice."

Under such circumstances, a collaboration acquires many of the features of psychotherapy, especially emotional catharsis. For those who doubt that poetry has value in our daily lives, I recommend collaboration as a way to dialogue about important or unresolved issues. Writing *Beyond Our Control* was my most intense experience of collaboration, and it also helped me work through the loss of a great friend.

9. Compatibility

As in any task involving more than one person, the wheels of poetic collaboration are lubricated by compatibility between the participants. There are several different kinds of compatibility, including stylistic, thematic, tempermental, intellectual and moral. The more of these held in common, the greater the compatibility. Paradoxically, tension is also important. A fine balance can sometimes produce a unique work of literature.

10. Process vs. Product Orientation

Product is clearly dependent on process in a collaboration. This is not different from individual writing, but in a collaboration the value of trusting the creative process is more obvious. Writing without a planned ending is more exploratory and exciting than writing pre-conceived, set pieces.

Conclusion

These are just a few of the many factors that play into a poetic collaboration. The possibilities are nearly endless, given the vast range of poetic styles, subjects and personalities among poets.

Heterogeneous matches produce the most distinctive and exploratory third voices while also stimulating adaptive growth in the participants. Because it is also a social act, collaboration can also be deeply satisfying in a way that individual writing might not. It is also a form of creative play that can rejuvenate a poet's creative flow. Collaboration expands the potential of poetry.

My Collaborators

Harry Smith (1936 - 2012)
Harry Smith was the founder/editor/director of The Smith Press and the founder/director of the Generalist Association and the *Generalist Papers*. The Smith Press published more than 70 titles over five decades. He also established *Pulpsmith* (a literary quarterly) which published hundreds of poets. Smith was a co-founder and twice President of COSMEP. He received PEN Center's Medwick Award "for his poetry, his commitment to human values, and his achievements as an editor" and the Small Press Center's Poor Richard Award for lifetime achievement. Smith was the author of thirteen published books of poetry and three books of collected essays.
Period of Collaboration: February, 2006 - November, 2006

John Elsberg (1945 - 2012)
John Elsberg was a poet, reviewer, editor, and historian. He was the host of open poetry readings at The Writer's Center in Bethesda, Maryland, for almost twenty-five years. Elsberg was the fiction editor of *Gargoyle* and the editor/poetry editor of *Bogg, The Delmarva Review*, and *Delaware Poetry Review*. He authored over a dozen books and chapbooks of poetry.
Period of Collaboration: May, 2007 - July, 2012

Hugh Fox (1932 - 2011)
Hugh Fox, Ph.D., was a Professor Emeritus at Michigan State University. He was a founding member of the Pushcart Prize and was also on the founding board of COSMEP. Fox edited the avant-garde litmag *Ghost Dance* during the sixties. He was a contributing reviewer for *Pulpsmith, Choice* and *SPR* and among others. Fox received three Fulbright Professorships to universities in Central and South America. Fox was the author of over sixty-two books, including books on anthropology, poetry, short fiction, and many novels. He was one of the most widely published poets in America.
Period of Collaboration: April, 2009 - April, 2010

Glenna Luschei (1932 -)
Glenna Luschei is a poet, publisher and translator. She is the publisher of Solo Press and its magazine series *Café Solo, Solo Café*, and *Solo Novo*. She was the first woman President of COSMEP. Luschei has been the recipient of fellowships from the National Endowment for the Arts and D.H. Lawrence. She was given an

Honorary Doctorate of Literature from St. Andrew's Presbyterian College (Laurinburg, NC) and a Master of Life Award from The University of Nebraska. Luschei earned her Ph.D. in Hispanic Languages and Literature from the University of California at Santa Barbara. She is the author of more than two dozen books.
Period of Collaboration: January, 2013 - August, 2015

Alison Stone (1964 -   )
Alison Stone has an MFA, Creative Writing from Pine Manor College. Her first collection, *They Sing at Midnight*, won the 2003 Many Mountains Moving Poetry Award. She is the recipient of *Poetry's* Frederick Bock Prize and the *New York Quarterly's* Madeline Sadin Award. Stone is the author of four collections of poetry.
Period of Collaboration: February, 2014 - April, 2017

Eric Greinke was born in 1948 in Grand Rapids, Michigan. He first saw publication at the age of fourteen after winning a high school literary contest. He was educated at Grand Valley State University, with a B.A. in English and Psychology, and a M.S.W. in Clinical Social Work. Following his service in the U.S. Coast Guard, he published *Earth Songs* (1970), his first chapbook of poems. As a young poet, he studied with poets Robert Bly and Ted Berrigan, and had poet Donald Hall as a mentor. Since then, he has produced numerous collections of poetry, a novel, a fishing book, two essay collections, a translation of Rimbaud, a collection of interviews and a collection of poetry criticism. His poems, essays, reviews and fiction have been published widely in the U.S. and abroad in hundreds of literary magazines and newspapers, such as *the Aurorean, California Quarterly, The Delaware Poetry Review, Gargoyle, Ginyu* (Japan), *The Green Door* (Belgium), *The Hurricane Review, The Journal* (UK), *Main Street Rag*, the *New York Quarterly,* the *Paterson Literary Review, The Pedestal Magazine, Poem, Prosopisia* (India), *Schuylkill Valley Journal, The South Carolina Review* and *The University of Tampa Review*. His poems have been translated into several languages, and included in two international anthologies. As a literary activist, he has worked for the Michigan Artists In The Schools Program, taught poetry writing at the experimental Grand Rapids City High School, edited or published numerous collections of poetry by a wide variety of his fellow American poets and   collaborated with many of his contemporaries. Further details may be found on his website www.ericgreinke.com.

from Presa Press

John Amen
> *At The Threshold Of Alchemy;* ISBN: 978-0-9800081-5-9; 86 pgs.; $13.95.

Guy Beining
> *Nozzle 1-36;* Chapbook; 40 pgs.; $6.00.

Louis E. Bourgeois
> *Alice*; Chapbook; 40 pgs.; $6.00.

Alan Catlin
> *Walking Among Tombstones in the Fog*; ISBN: 978-0-9965026-4-1; 72 pgs.; $13.95.

David Chorlton
> *Bird On A Wire*; ISBN: 978-0-9965026-5-8; 68 pgs.; $13.95.

Kirby Congdon
> *Selected Poems & Prose Poems;* ISBN: 978-0-9772524-0-4; 84 pgs.; $15.00.
>
> *Athletes*;* ISBN: 978-0-9831251-0-5; 52 pgs.; $9.95.
>
> *Remarks And Reflections - Essays*[†]; ISBN: 978-0-9888279-5-0; 96 pgs.; $17.95.
>
> *Kirby Congdon: 65 Years Of Poetry - A Bibliography of His Poems, Prose Poems and Criticism*; ISBN: 978-0-9888279-0-5; 132 pgs.; $20.00

Hugh Fox
> *Blood Cocoon - Selected Poems Of Connie Fox;* ISBN: 978-0-9740868-9-7; 72 pgs.; $15.00.
>
> *Time & Other Poems*; Chapbook; 44 pgs.; $6.00.

Eric Greinke
> *The Drunken Boat & Other Poems From The French Of Arthur Rimbaud;* ISBN: 978-0-9772524-7-3; 108 pgs.; $15.95.
>
> *The Potential Of Poetry*[†]; ISBN: 978-0-9831251-1-2; 88 pgs.; $11.95.
>
> *Conversation Pieces - Selected Interviews*; ISBN: 978-0-9831251-6-7; 100 pgs.; $15.95.
>
> *For The Living Dead - New & Selected Poems*[†]; ISBN: 978-0-9888279-2-9; 160 pgs.; $15.95.
>
> *Poets In Review;* ISBN: 978-0-9965026-0-3; 124 pgs.; $15.95.
>
> *Zen Duende - Collaborative Poems* (w/ Glenna Luschei); ISBN: 978-0-9965026-1-0; 64 pgs.; $13.95.

Ruth Moon Kempher
> *Retrievals*[†]; ISBN: 978-0-9888279-8-1; 68 pgs.; $15.95.

Kerry Shawn Keys
> *The Burning Mirror**; ISBN: 978-0-9772524-9-7; 92 pgs.; $14.95.
>
> *Book Of Beasts**; ISBN: 978-0-9800081-4-2; 64 pgs.; $12.95.
>
> *Transporting, A Cloak Of Rhapsodies*;* ISBN: 978-0-9800081-8-0;

Night Flight*; ISBN: 978-0-9831251-3-6; 96 pgs.; $15.95.

Arthur Winfield Knight

High Country; Chapbook; 32 pgs.; $6.00.

Champagne Dawns; Chapbook; 28 pgs.; $6.00.

Richard Kostelanetz

PO/EMS; Chapbook; 40 pgs.; $6.00.

More Fulcra Poems; Chapbook; 52 pgs.; $6.00.

Purling Sonnets; Chapbook; 32 pgs.; $6.00.

Linda Lerner

Living In Dangerous Times; Chapbook; 56 pgs.; $6.00.

Donald Lev

Only Wings - 20 Poems Of Devotion; Chapbook; 28 pgs.; $6.00.

Where I Sit [†]; ISBN: 978-0-9888279-9-8; 88 pgs.; $15.95.

Lyn Lifshin

In Mirrors; ISBN: 978-0-9772524-3-5; 84 pgs.; $15.00.

Lost Horses; Chapbook; 36 pgs.; $6.00.

Gerald Locklin

From A Male Perspective; Chapbook; 32 pgs.; $6.00.

Deep Meanings - Selected Poems 2008-2013; ISBN: 978-0-9831251-9-8; 132 pg.; $16.95.

Peter Ludwin

Rumors Of Fallible Gods; ISBN: 978-0-9831251-8-1; 108 pgs.; $15.95.

Glenna Luschei

Seedpods; Chapbook; 40 pgs.; $6.00.

Total Immersion; ISBN: 978-0-9800081-0-4; 96 pgs.; $15.00.

Witch Dance - New & Selected Poems; ISBN: 978-0-9800081-7-3; 84 pgs.; $13.95.

Sprouts; Chapbook; 28 pgs.; $6.00.

Leaving It All Behind; ISBN: 978-0-9831251-2-9; 104 pgs.; $15.95.

Gary Metras

The Moon In The Pool [†]; ISBN: 978-0-9888279-7-4; 68 pgs.; $12.95.

Stanley Nelson

Pre-Socratic Points & Other New Poems*; ISBN: 978-0-9772524-4-2; 84 pgs.; $15.00.

Limbos For Amplified Harpsichord*; ISBN: 978-0-9772524-8-0; 144 pgs.; $17.95.

City Of The Sun*; ISBN: 978-0-9800081-2-8; 126 pgs.; $15.95.

B. Z. Niditch

Captive Cities; Chapbook; 36 pgs.; $8.00.

Roseanne Ritzema, Ed.

Inside The Outside - An Anthology Of Avant- Garde American Poets*; ISBN: 978-0-9772524-1-8; 304 pgs.; $29.95.

Poetry Matters - A Collection Of Essays; ISBN: 978-0-9965026-3-4; 110 pgs.; $13.95.

Lynne Savitt

The Deployment Of Love In Pineapple Twilight; Chapbook; 48 pgs.; $6.00.

Steven Sher

Grazing On Stars - Selected Poems; ISBN: 978-0-9831251-7-4; 84 pgs.; $15.95.

Harry Smith

Up North (w/ Eric Greinke); Chapbook; 40 pgs.; $6.00.

Little Things*; ISBN: 978-0-9800081-3-5; 78 pgs.; $13.95.

t. kilgore splake

Ghost Dancer's Dreams*; ISBN: 978-0-9831251-4-3; 68 pgs.; $12.95.

Coming Home; Chapbook; 36 pgs.; $6.00.

Splake Fishing In America*; ISBN: 978-0-9888279-1-2; 614 pgs.; $20.00.

Beyond The Ghosts; Chapbook; 36 pgs.; $6.00.

Winter River Flowing - Selected Poems 1979-2014[†]; ISBN: 978-0-9888279-6-7; 152 pgs.; $21.95.

Tommy's Desk; ISBN: 978-0-9965026-2-7; 64 pages; $13.95.

Alison Stone

Dangerous Enough[†]; ISBN: 978-0-9888279-3-6; 80 pgs.; $15.95.

Lloyd Van Brunt

Delirium - Selected Poems; Chapbook; 48 pgs.; $6.00.

Marine Robert Warden

Beyond The Straits*; ISBN: 978-0-980001-6-6; 72 pgs.; $13.95.

Leslie H. Whitten Jr.

The Rebel - Poems By Charles Baudelaire; Chapbook; 48 pgs.; $7.00.

A. D. Winans

The Other Side Of Broadway - Selected Poems; ISBN: 978-0-9772524-5-9; 132 pgs.; $18.00.

Wind On His Wings; Chapbook; 44 pgs.; $8.00.

This Land Is Not My Land [†]; ISBN: 978-0-9888279-4-3; 60 pgs.; $14.95.

* currently out of print
[†] available as e-book through amazon.com

**Available through Baker & Taylor,
The Book House, Coutts Information Services,
Midwest Library Services, local bookstores
& directly from the publisher - www.presapress.com**

**Exclusive European distribution through Gazelle Book
Services, Ltd. - www.gazellebookservices.co.uk**